DET
O
NAT
ED
MIR
ROR

ALSO BY SARA LARSEN

All Revolutions Will Be Fabulous,
Printing Press, 2014

Merry Hell, Atelos, 2016

The Riot Grrrl Thing, Roof Books, 2019

DET O NAT ED MIR ROR

SAR A LA R SEN

THE ELEPHANTS

Published 2023 by The Elephants
Printed in the United States
Author photo by Michael Jeffrey Lee
The text of this book is set
in FreightText Pro and Helvetica Neue

23 24 25 26 27 5 4 3 2 1

First Edition

ISBN 978-1-988979-47-2 (print) and
978-1-988979-48-9 (ebook)

Library of Congress Control Number 2022944340

for Michael Jeffrey Lee

CONTENTS

[MY SECRET BODY] : 3

VEGA : 5

DETONATED MIRROR : 6

MY MOON BODY HAS : 7

CINDER TWIN : 8

is it all about fleeing gutted time
make love with the cursor : 9

RATTLER : 10

I kill the deer it gleams
as prayer disappears : 11

DESERT EVE FOR W. : 12

[MY SECRET BODY] : 13

THE CORAL DREAM : 15

THE SPOONS : 16

there will be nothing there : 17

LETTER FROM E.D. : 18

[MY SECRET BODY] : 19
the demon appeared as
a complex constellation : 20
BARDO : 21
[MY SECRET BODY] : 22
THE FUR APPARITION : 23
LITTLE RAT MOON : 24
THE REALM OF LEOPARD : 25
as of late I've had fire in my throat : 26
[MY SECRET BODY] : 27
DOUBLE EXILE : 28
THE SEA IN THE HEATH : 29
what's more true than sleep : 30
SOLAR ECLIPSE : 31
[MY SECRET BODY] : 32
a likeness passes melts
an exhalation of former : 34
CANOPY : 35
SLEPT & SLEPT : 36
unfuckable revenue streams
is that what you want? : 37
MILK'S MOON ANIMAL : 38
BLUE NEPTUNE : 39

my jaws are lazuli
lotus flowers, violet : 40

INTERVIEW WITH THE SUN : 41

[MY SECRET BODY] : 42

I question my own dreams,
they are emissaries : 44

YOU DISAPPEAR SINGING : 45

ŠIROKÁ : 46

THE ORB : 47

sextiled by spiders : 48

ONLY AN EYE : 49

EVENINGS AND MORNINGS : 50

I don't wanna suffer intolerably
with no respite : 51

IN THE LINE OF LEO : 52

[MY SECRET BODY] : 53

HAWK : 54

CROWN OF MIRRORS : 55

some of us got old some
of us waned in existence : 56

ANIMALES : 57

ropes that bind : 58

THE CANAL : 59

MARSHLAND : 60

hotter than death like
a rattle I'm soaked : 61

THE TREE : 62

BONE EXTRACT : 63

TRUST IN THE CODE : 65

horrors a heart the cigarette
smoke an IUD : 67

[MY SECRET BODY] : 68

there shall be no more cakes,
black moon motorcycle : 69

BIRD'S DESTROYER : 70

FRAILTY : 71

[MY SECRET BODY] : 73

what will we have when we look up : 74

THE EATER : 75

[MY SECRET BODY] : 77

OPEN SILENCE : 78

meaning the whole sphere
I said licking : 80

KILL A THING I WANT : 81

LETTER AGAINST DISTANCE : 83

[MY SECRET BODY] : 85

. . . . .

the moon has the dawn in it

it does break the world

   syncopates what’s invisible

      sub rosa

. . . .

DET

O

NAT

ED

MIR

ROR

[MY SECRET BODY]

My secret body has a plan for me and it is a wild one.

In the navel of my secret body grows a phosphorescent dream. This dream is made of honey and gently stokes the underlimbs of the desert's dry palette. Not knowing how to travel the earth, rooted in imperceptibility, I am half-asleep with embers, remembering my longing heart. I dream of leathered embryos who are omniscient and without a mouth, but enunciate clearly and with conviction: *If my secret body is not there,* I *don't want to be there.*

It is said that we are in love with each other even in the womb. It is said that on my wings I bring air to you in those underlimb canyons. From being nothing somewhere, something final and small, the Sun plunges us reconstructed in the walking air. Disorderly, I shoulder you back to bewilderment.

Fast forward the videotape (and watch the seizured lines that cross the screen): it is my secret body who gilds me luminously as I turn through states, who sends bulls onto absurd epiphany roads, who buries branchlike pee into lace forest grounds and florals my boots and thongs with urine. It is my secret body who stores water wells in the trunk. In endless circles, I am mistress to the governance of the horned owl and bowls of smoking burnt up wooded cauldrons. As I drive on, my humiliations become quite pitiless and brutal, as if a spell has enjambed me. I see I am now missing my torso, and I see that it has returned. And yet, at another turn, my fingers mist over and my palms appear to guide the wheel. When my larynx is present, I cling to beating song.

My secret body watches me and moves me and shocks me and holds me, covers me in blackness, in blankets. I shift in its undulations—what else could I do?

VEGA

scorpion salted smoke
extinguished hair
drop of bone
  the meadows
faux hyacinths, faux lavender, broom

twisted out heather
reaper valley sprawl
mounted limbs
thin leather winds   mother serpent winds
struck violin skins

DETONATED MIRROR

faucet sockets
purple consciousness cactus, fat blood clot boneyard row

dominion needs an author, vertebrae punches out of Dirt of
the Dead
mesquite and needles to cancel skin's net, tethered with ice
limbs in
bedrock of rose quartz, PO Box, syringe
star circuit, animal rain droplets, cartilage horns, mouths of
scorpions

wheels of bespangled dust where I weep
I guess we're in
rhizomic consciousness, was
lover of nightmare,
doors

MY MOON BODY HAS

my moon body has
four faces
they generate each other so
I can't really see
they gush into shape
unknown, dimensionless
like a sword & a scissor

they kiss dispossession
wear piles of dead
lilies & snakeshead

I am a phantom river
I am an unpolished spoon

CINDER TWIN

ides of deer
grate the eves   bodice paw

buttercream spotted
tip of gun
cinder twin
hearts
me barbed
wire
threaded with furs
I won't sleep with a skull
specks   command amber open only to me
pass thru veins

like all sands
sink the rot---   I mean, Rocks
deeper plea
beloved knees

is it all about fleeing gutted time make love with the cursor
blinking penniless I draw to me certain selves knotted asteroids
seclude me longing is in the body words dimensionless they doctor
the gap slowly I lick my lips my hair scented with warpaint
this tissue-y vortex curls towards me a quadrillion buttered vulvas
I'm careless with intestines, devour all curtained things
just like that I am a snakebite
embodiment of sedition
I sing hot grief down the drain
I go commando an unwounded creature eating butchers
with shunted knife
one leg of fragility
what will you do my Lumbered Ejaculate but lay down and dream
may I realize a quality infinite to you
abracadabra nothing concrete my vulgarity hysteric a novel that
fucking falls apart such as all beings and rando things

RATTLER

blue new moon
                    Ecstatic bluefish
  I told you I am copper
  I do not hunt or adorn desert plank
born a transient winged unprepared pillow

I acknowledge you as a man
        hired by sequitur
  forgive how I cruise
            breaking midnight hair

thronged by phantom stare
I stopped my Hopes
      with bliss they fled
vellum rattler must be fed

I kill the deer it gleams as prayer disappears
on hand robbed of succor, somnambulant
blood on tile, write space of sleep, water shape
of jaguar at rest, I board his macroscopic gaze
cornered fur, spots of budded blood, from
non-understanding I am dug into earth, five
fathoms below scoured heliotropic
personality, rough red paws dig upwards
not one swearword
or gasp
for fallen things disappear not in discourse but loam

DESERT EVE FOR W.

in snow white sand
  I caught yr hair of rain
thunder grew
        rocks flew down

 I held those spider webs
  my fingers became threads
                    my needled
                    hands sore &
                      open blue

seas crashed from briars
ships pirated hungry skyfolds
    the desert was still / water oblivion

  strands
 & strands of mirror

[MY SECRET BODY]

Wailing under a drunken starfield near the mammoth cactus, I feel I am an aurora cloud inundating with black pellets the salty mesa. I miss the magnetic delegations of earth, the scattered limbs of my corpus, which lay shredded and hidden elsewhere. I feel I am imprisoned here, overwhelmed with a disappearing and reappearing physicality, half sentient, half ephemeral, like a rough ghost.

I hold binder's thread, black and waxed. It dangles from my tremorous hands. This is despair. I don't even have a needle! How do I stitch? I take another brackish sip of liquor. The heart-shaped moon dwindles down like a dead flame.

Suddenly I am a snail, a mollusk, a candied form on earthen shape. The thread and the liquor splay and splatter in the animal's cool night. In this array, the earth (like me) contracts and expands. The sky is full of fire-mouthed wolves and fly trap birthed coyotes. The world, lumpen and fat. My body without any limbs at all, or they are no longer visible. The cosmos boiled down and ladled out. At the same time it's exorbitantly full, immodest, a multiverse of sniffling, itchy, pus-dry beings roiled together, and a gleaming tornado of slippery ones too—compact yet infinite, dead, living and at thresholds. It is mineral, soluble, inebriating. No one being sees through to another side, if any side existed. My thread is everywhere and therefore hopeless to control. I am waylaid in a curtain of foundation.

THE CORAL DREAM

if I were you I'd become a Deer
        before the Coral dream
  drapes sperm with   surf

I wake up to no commands
Lest the orchid sky were
                    omnipotent
swerveless bone

        the key of C is gone
            sighing
          like breath

  Curriculum

THE SPOONS

branches blue turn none
rose blood mount
 the spoons
   lick two cup marrow this bone

 some
Invisible
stalk Cactus bit   I'm one of it
it's kind   not pinyon but spread pinch
 inner thigh needle
juniper
winds may exist

can I survive
        second name

glyph foot hive   turn none
 no one

there will be nothing there
my season is gem consciousness, rose, bee
syllable gauzy a cobweb wheel of space, my own
beings' center mute again, a seldom tooth left by
door, me visible in the haze, saffron owls
flicker oblivion midnight,
declaimed water, simple things unweb unwind a little
tuft of fur ruffle in wind
earthworms, loop of sunset, unhemmed capacity, letters

LETTER FROM E.D.

I too have
afterbirth pages
a state of silvery copenhagen blue
texts & letters to me
are in the overgrowth
earthly sugar
not a virgin of chaos
but
dissimulated

I do not fuck Eagles
I underscore Feathers
& Flight
the lunar desert
mumbling a witch-flower

Emily goes,
The Universe is Yours

[MY SECRET BODY]

A *cry of rapture and horror*. It is a shock to see so much barbed wire. I had expected alien canyons, filigrees of open bone rock, a mouthed earth that might engulf the premium of *me*. But arriving in the Southern Wheel, it is barbed wire that defines the land. Barbed plants, bustles of knives, suggest that their pointed nude bodies were at some point twisted by myopic concepts such as enclosure to scald the land. Prison shape. As for me, the falconless barbed wire contracts my expansion South.

the demon appeared as a complex constellation
I want to know where its blood is, transcend mutterance
annihilation a pronoun I think I inhabit another fleshful door my
shoulder all redwood effable panting my solar shifting humanity
unhinge from my spinal place these mobs of voice
it resembles an odyssey remember I stole all the fires and
I didn't know what to wear
my thighs shook in remembrance
pelted back to the present we hover in a place with no floor no walls
no way to curdle up in star chains or for me to find the laced
corset I used to own
last time I had my period you were fisting me in the backseat of my car
demons are in layers, tissue, cycle spellbound by repair of staccato "self"
demon says,
I'd like to be more vulnerable than this for you.
Meticulously vulnerable. Epistemologically vulnerable. Luxe, unclenched, movable, an amalgam of organs and veins and fascia and nervous systems all piled up like luxury bracelets, all stretched out like old cotton thongs

BARDO

I walk through smoke rings
barbed   cut   blood
every cloud a gun

sometimes I have another face another lips
    coyotes howl like another voice
  or barn owls
I'm in a semi-circle of mountains

dragon ghosts in vista

[MY SECRET BODY]

To see the name on the phone, inside the car, inside the desert. To see the name on the phone in the cabin at the table. To see the name on the phone at the intersection of town, at the gas station, at the rest stop, to see the name on the phone as I lay awake in bed or as I awaken in bed. To see the name on the phone as I am adjacent to the horse field. To see the name on the phone as I pull up the hill and pass the Virgin de Guadalupe. To see the name on the phone as I finish writing in the white five subject notebook. To see the name on the phone as I gather my reserves. To see the name on the phone as I splay with the sunlight. To see the name on the phone as I become animal shifting quietly through indexed grass. To see the name on the phone as a garret, double-edged with lost bottoms. To see the name on the phone as the pyramid caesura of touch. To see the name on the phone scattered and culled. To see the name on the phone of imperious destiny, the secret door.

THE FUR APPARITION

hung cow sewer I obviously
  Came fanged Fate   among
 wisps, fleeting tails the Fur
apparition
lonely as my neighing
Lover
my time twilight no Other time for
a carcass like Me
smoke ghost
  fingernail opus

LITTLE RAT MOON

little Rat Moon
spit   hailstones
from her loom

procreates Half of me
cleaves the starry haloed
eye   as glass becomes water
as all things suck up

THE REALM OF LEOPARD

Like ash
    the realm
            of leopard
ghosts pollenate themselves

twisted in agapanthus
  bee pigeon fulcrum moon

the curve uneasy, uneternal

I was with you,   you Faun
and in ways without you—
  Floods mouthed
    bewitched
projected
      silver shafts

Wind hung on the door
emerald gauze
funereal fuzz of nerve

the cottoned chest is a Letter

as of late I've *had fire in my throat*
from which I drank water a tongue   alone even with all of your manifold defects,
you are my Lady   I've had bad luck but great honesty
for meat and love remember me as god to you, the greatest pussy
so much I am in debt
wayward sepulcher into base death with a sore behind
repressed by kings I've become food   sleeping in the grotto or in barrels
sausages breaking upon a starved crew

[MY SECRET BODY]

My secret body grows wild grasses from the eyeballs. My secret body has such a face that is constantly erased or rearranged. You may say my secret body has numerous faces, or perhaps no face at all. My secret body has a mask and the wax drips into their mouths. My secret body always is tasting wax on their lips and tongue and throat. I'm confused. My secret body has whispers fly through the air and they appear like singes of feathery spit that heat dance.

Turtle Mountain has advice for me. My boots relax on an overturned cardboard box. I say to Turtle Mountain, *do I already have my secret body?* Turtle Mountain puts their porous blood-clotted face close to mine. *Why do you cleave words into slices when you are a chain?* I nodded, *You're right.* I feel slightly embarrassed because I don't understand. Before dread Turtle Mountain, I pretend I do.

DOUBLE EXILE

I follow double exile
    earthen synapse
my falcon eye must sleep
tufted theater unfolded lands
no where for hands like these—

Asleep in insoluble wing
    luminous orbits blood the season
      the hair is stitched in
    circumference of Bird
            no map to distance
    dream abducts the dead

THE SEA IN THE HEATH

the sea in the heath
I cry when blood dries up
        nebula flora   language
of building death
      modern hands
            river of eyes

I cry when   I saw
 a bear made of horse hair
sunspot with glimmering gaseous
        mane
        dissolves dust-quick
              never
                    made form

what's more true than sleep
a sea-bridge amethyst in fathoms
I wash the violets from my crashing hair, catch strands in
netted waves, they bury themselves like clams
teeth ecstatic, I was making love as a pigeon
who steals high-minded glass, reminded your name has muscle,
I was making love as a vial of poison, lassitude, from my lips looses
a pearl, a bird nest painfully pinned to ground, it is luminous to be
in air and in disorder, on the surface I was singing
as my body meanwhile undrunkenly rolled back

SOLAR ECLIPSE

stellar winds move me
sleepy sex diamond of self-same voice
there is a ghost in my bath
conceptually aggregate

my weird is not owned, it is north
eclipsed in weapon blue, my flesh

doesn’t know   devoured barefoot double
flyers of strawed light

[MY SECRET BODY]

Mycelium is the fruit of my secret body, its loss is the loss of all things organic dust dry and decomposite, the white bone nopales withered in the sticks, the razored mouse burnished on the henequen spear.

My secret body is in perpetual conjugal visit with all sexing variety, oak ripe moss, softcore ground layer, sediment roiling in waxen waters and the heaping sky who groans like pressurized glass in the hot black hole.

Gnostic mycelium is the earthen fruit of my secret body who is self-pursuing, poly-plasticene and volcanic with ash.

The Losses forgotten and engraved in wildfire libraries, *they who were not here* written and written again by my secret body.

Mycelium is the fruit of my secret body who rampages secretly like soft duvet cover underground, where secret rivers contain all the folded notes of invented time, nutrients of the fungal body.

The fungal body is a discography of skeletal piping, routes in sedentary fascia, it harnesses visits from those who are past and winds avenues through fecund undergarments of pomegranate play nights.

In the theater of my secret body's mycelium interstates, the Feathered mourn in dignity against the timetables of secular trains.

In the codex of the fungal body all souls are a spinal tap,

the opera of their empty carcass is in seizure beneath the pine canopy.

Coded mycelium is the fruit of my secret body. It lays prone in the annexed mold of anonymous supine insects, legs slackened helplessly up. They sing in their death a nutrient spasm.

It is the tension rod of carpal space, whose routes project those who are past.

In the vast, tethered net of the fungal body, there is my secret body.

a likeness passes melts an exhalation of former
selves my words say dangerous things: "love" "enter"
"mirror" "heat" smudged with self-display I wanna be a
little slit memories washed out low-rent the credits
roll by sustained by telling this story
dunno what you'll make of it, when I'm writing I don't care
if she loves me or doesn't love me who cares
we pretended we lived
intermission was a bitch *bardos* of orgasms I don't want to leave
smoked out by my own ghastly smoke
texts come and I must read them ringing and beeping they don't
leave a girl alone
gimme your palms across the waters, things as we think they are
contract tremble
contract   honeysuckle hands

CANOPY

roses in the rain
  dream of
        sucking yr blood

no more
    craters of youth
          ilk at my back
 canopy of leather
          bee & jackrabbit
    in unison—

eunuch brought me here
        under stars
      bloodmaster

SLEPT & SLEPT

vomitorium crystal springs
 they crowd me with distress
last night I was a pyre
 came to in a lock phase
cold waters corneas scaled
 in my breast
my own face was my lover
 the breath an equal room

4 Roses in death strip —
darkness ameliorates no sun
wisps silvered consciousness
 elaborates string music
slept & slept until money was no more

the science of loving was a bailiff, a bird

tomato disintegrating pain on the floorboard
 to hold without seizure

unfuckable revenue streams is that what you want?
your death will go uncreated, roll the voice into sand
cannot liberate delusion and become the competition
one grey day I woke up eager ensconced by reality's tremor film
became like a convoluted dirty old street
selected with fire its jolt narrative components

voice memo on Friday in love with emanation
interruption

lick me across spectrum merchant in vertigo interior
across entropy buildings scaffolding towns wardrobes grails
lick me across certain planets that share their blood
across beauty reasoning and language

was blue form of beautiful horse was reborn as tree of bone
the boundaries of breath know no shrinking nor folding chairs

MILK'S MOON ANIMAL

milk's moon animal
    a cosmogony   Lover's
                                        face
          self-immolates
                      unpoisoned as honeybees shrunken
on my neck

you shall not touch the bull
hunkered in Amber lanced with Name
    vacancy is

  earthborn primal light scissor
cow's pink pained squirt
                      ungutted by barbed
wire

without signature

BLUE NEPTUNE

blue neptune swept up
        the gods everywhere

a furnace whose cyclonic heat
   streams jeweled entropy

there is a Great Dark Spot on earth too
  primal wings
         affix
        as
      threads
rattlesnakes and the dead

delirious wind   and paper rain

my jaws are lazuli lotus flowers, violet
with honey drops, eaten by swords on
swarming fish-heaped swells, I speak only
cross-eyed, hung rightsidedown my lord
I am just a mammalian monsoon, no other
freak
just want of rain with my sapphired breath
I blow winged exoskeletons unsouled from my bed
   just like that
I am a steward of obfuscation, of cross-garters
malarias
I'll do my best
to resurrect doubt from hideous soil

INTERVIEW WITH THE SUN

tentacle purple,   silver bee asleep
wrapped in apex fleece & two men of prose
all that wilts   a button under
rosehip tongue
        solemn wind catches you there—

I am so far from home
          in interview with the sun
my glass bod shatters
   the balm in ugly moat
it's but an arroyo
            quartz & turquoise
flooded retrievable lips
      sweet sod armpits

tho I can't see them   headland
                          Eternity
        snakes
     have not face
                  but holes in the ground

[MY SECRET BODY]

Location: locust sheets / unpublished interview. Surrounded by a scorpion, a bird, a sow, they question me and note my responses in the grimoires of their particular species. I never see their notes, nor do I expect to. Here is my recording, made on cassette, which I replay:

Scorpion: *What is my secret body?*
MY secret body flies to me the way an animal comes when you are still IT simply appears LIMBS and organs and nerves and tissue and detritus as skin and teeth and mucus and bones are spouted from a blood vein, a tempestuous dust rag on the wrist of the planet STALAGMITES in throated caves, canyons leeched of sound, aching murder bees solemnly pollinating the invented universe, FLIES relentlessly shimmy in my ear and unbutton their visibility (invisible) when I turn to face them SOUNDS without carriers, they are false bears playing in the steep hillside BE careful of distraction, do not slip down this steep hillside you came to cry on, this rock isn't so secure and the nettle and thistle will just watch OVERLOOK the rough dead

Bird: *In the dream of words, do you wipe tears or collide in phrases of laughter? Are you able to* TALK *to anyone?? Without a mouth, without lips?*

NO way to answer that question, I cannot say, WORDS peel away imprisoned desiccated NO funds to reinstate them, nothing to congeal them MY bottom chirping and chattering MOUTH is fire CASTS mummies in swaggering play TERRIBLE wicked thoughts think themselves IMMEDIATELY I omnisciently tinsel the sick, ballast the dead, MAY I please taste a drink near cougar den, flooded monsoon creek bed NIGHT is fallen, I am glad I have, if not a mouth, at least a hole of light

Sow: *Our next question is personal. Are you able to jailbreak and caress . . . do you have sexual meetings? If so, are they poignant, cursory or?*

DESERT dweller leans into spidery corners all night long POEMS I write and write and write WORDS sing like grasshoppers AMULETS via text or email SET detached bones RABBIT eye with such and such a name MY secret body fills with carbonation, shakes explosive upon receipt ACROSS I feel it LETTERS grow fingernails, dig deep inside me, fist me, unencumbered limbs and lips WASH over with sunlight arsenic flint of larger fishing net, FULL of mirrors.

LOVE letters are the letters of the day RETURN address is often blurred or splotched out, as if someone had spilt milk all over it, WARM milk I welcome with my tongue, I think of nothing but next letters

I *question my own dreams, they are emissaries*
I question my birth this apartment my rosette-ish transposition
I have conscious pricks with your name racing like emperors
transfixed I sit around and daydream and cum in this common
place lyric altar
I am creating the universe
puckered up I am invisible axle my characters so guilty
a delegation with luxury, queer with lace, in my dreams
I'm for sale, slick and untended, in my dreams
I'm a young one none of this ever happened

YOU DISAPPEAR SINGING

you disappear singing
and I in a sky of fingertips
cracking in flame
woolen—wet fur of stringy labyrinth
unknown home made of wind
at least I found Pasolini's book
and the fountains continue
to piss

votive womb
the brutal province of Light
familiar to the Bound

nothing will be unknown to me
nothing exalted
body hair chest
the snowcapped eye and I
a flycatch

ŠIROKÁ

the threshold is infinite
    exists in mouth palette of
        snake

unknown in my guts is the moon
  and Jupiter burning its heart

I wanted to return
    in naked language
  the alchemy of waste
  the surrealism of love
    who shifts atypically gnosis

it is common to stay up all night
 milky way I find my body
    flickers I lose what
 painters call "perspective"

THE ORB

sheets of glass style my face
I was a wave
generating mouthfuls of deadly piss

and
then I burnt up
ashes erect
gilded with roughness,

astronomical clock

void, --

I hone the rites of Incompleteness
the gnostic *terma* of your body
enjoyed in correspondence

to remake social order with
orbs of
phenomena
flame

sextiled by spiders
my fingernails a balmy cave
delectable mossy
ends & tendrils flare out your bay eyes are
in their luminescent phase, in their
                                        liberating grove
hand in sockets, my consort without reason,
protectors purify time of things-to-let-go-of,
that certain silhouette hands me
birds of efficacy NO MORE FOR ME these
unstated fathoms, I am crossed
by lunation, reckless/careless/feckless
drag sentience
liberation carries enjoyment body

ONLY AN EYE

the sun is already
my eclipse
the obscure Lion's moon
unemployed love
naked of color
all eras illuminated disc of koruna
the deathly edge
drowsy with fruit
I am façade
spectate—
torch stone
bridge black

EVENINGS AND MORNINGS

evenings and mornings
if not borne they disappear
the immoderate presence of the gate
at which myself is a thimble

cleft in underwear left by the sink
on the floor

splitting

trampled bread is a mystery
like language heard on the bridge
tended and rose
threshing fields

separation and revelation
sacred devotion

I don't wanna suffer intolerably with no respite
can I shake this life asking corpses about Being Broken
bankrupt dreams about a vulva
a magical corpse I drink Light from an unexpected
fiction embossed flowering sponge I got booted from Writing then
spoken forward by entropy to squat in a hole
an expenditure invented from this war of wanting when I'm
    writing I don't care
if she loves me or doesn't love me who cares
what if I kick aside vital incarnations swoop into next breath

IN THE LINE OF LEO

in the line of Leo
  I only know wind
        this swift incarnation

its dewy map
      pores pumiced in allusive
sorrows

in Fall we walk
in Summer disembowel the swampy
          west

I am a rag bleached in Light
I dream your hair
          in gangs of
      revelation—

the rough poem   the dusky canal

[MY SECRET BODY]

My secret body, I wish you'd call me up as I drive through desolate pigmentation. The hot white sky is outrageous. Parts of my body are made to be lost. I pull over to a gravel turn-around. Mounds of salt dot the earth. Cut fingernails, cut hair. Flakes of skin. Dandruff. Seared by rays.

I come here in suspension, unplanetary. Nuclear tests, the water well in the trunk. Gut bacteria, microbes. I wish my secret body would call up the secret of my secret body. Belie ceaselessly their own existence - human, physical, animal, microbial, fungal, not only a carbon, but subtle, restless, uneven, luminous.

Anyway, how could they call me?? Lone stallion, I have no cell reception. Roaming, moving, slithering, greasy. My hands full of thickets. Shapeshifting hurts. It is mid-day and yet: moonlight shimmer. Time wobbles when images change.

HAWK

my brains hit air
air's slim arrows
obscure
the pearl

on the balcony
we viewed the stars
obscurity clears
addressed to Earth
I recoil   unnumbered
uncontented   untold
duality of latitude
or long
limits my Dream

celestial ghosts they are
rudders
on the
silver sea
Blazing Dark
A Hawk who swoops
down on
me

CROWN OF MIRRORS

I am with you in a crown of mirrors
    molten inconstant   rhythms
                        &
                    ghosts
  unemployed of fear
            what a strange negation
the head will wear clothes
    mouth scandalous blades
      I walk home anciently
snake
unknown disciplines delight

          mourning
          the crude blue sky

some of us got old some of us waned in existence
soiled dove noir I will construct
a new boss I don't care if "I" all dissolves, my heart is flawed like
a chrysanthemum a shattered poetical theme I stand behind it with my
shifting perceptions
cut into blankness a creature from sorrow-charged page I've fucked
a goddamn lot, even in sickness, even among the ants and the tourists
I have something to tell you it's the medium of transmutation it's
possible I become a sensorium arc plied by multifarious voices
    I liberate
your warm prick seeing recast words in nature luscious atonal
the slutty dark is there ravenous for your birthday enjambs our birth
from every pore this quivering has truly made me a citizen a hybrid
half jailed human food asks no questions
I commit blood's sacrilege, chain-smoke dried up spit from mouths
    of dead
monsters
you know it, I know it
I'm just smoke

ANIMALES

taught to eat by the animals
  but were we animal
                    enough?

in a convex of disappeared season
  doorway made into it –
              stupendously without
  touch
    or
   phrase

      insufficiency of word

                  search to spot
                animal
weather: first snow
                 track blood
                        fled
                       singing

ropes that bind
a field guide to limping
my sunset thick wife
moves the sun far away
distance is caterpillar
my goblet's an anonymous storm
with evening pasted on streetlights
her name is dried up
carved into saddle
suddenly so trouble
suddenly so bum

THE CANAL

I once was the canal
dawns did deform

nevertheless I exist
thru Saturnine tableaux

whispers flare into consciousness
stone heart on fire becomes
spontaneous
heart on fire

Saturn's wall

MARSHLAND

guided by silver strand
        suddenly
   translucently
I tip on   planks of
        seasick conflagration
as if I could step thru scrim
    encapsulate your form
your flight   crepuscular ship tipping
  you must
speak the Name
      in wind
     the one that spells
Salted skin

hotter than death like a rattle I'm *soaked*
you see what I mean when my blood sputters forth
it looks good from here blank screed folds
gallows shutter seclusion sexful hurled across
living space
I'm a menace I know it as I glide out of air whispers
gutters precipitation of fingernails I say You're The Foam
You're The Fur ensconced in body's limpness
I was seized with your literature but
who the fuck was
I
I wandered slowly as a cow
disappeared on the mountain
some spit on my hands

THE TREE

my double is a
  ghost
whose house is laid on flowers
            perhaps Death assented
the divided gaze
      barely named

  but the twin cannot shut
the tree is the same way
its diadem moves so slow
  and birds swoop with terror

BONE EXTRACT

incandescent prodigious human
  it was not a deer
walks in self's similitude
        part one: underwater thrall
     vassal   fastened his horse
but Myself
         am sound
Bone Extract
              beyond name
                         text
                       variant
           buoyancy
             vapor

       was annihilation
          selected by
          enchanted powders
  beyond distance

all our removes
          are tragic root
   these darings are informal
              dead perceivers

shadowed by education
delineate years
cadence of
perceptibility

dangles at
the
Deceptive
wayward, wayward
a magic for reference

TRUST IN THE CODE

Monologue of frost fragment
part three: this note accompanies
arbitrary “trust in the code”
their cancelled name be mortal

all chance stands
a
Haunted House
language
no longer possession
but
concealed in the Fawn
learner and founder
forgetter eraser

not robbed
flight
precursor moon
never deny me Madonna’s
memoir opaque delusive idle disk
subtracting
our possession a sovereign
suggests forget

what deed supersedes
silence?

where soldiers
cross
my red forced feet
A FLINT
thumb on the sea
strange feelings, indeed

horrors a heart the cigarette smoke an IUD
wolfbane mindful wolves, rats of
care, stones, am I going into exile or pointless skeleton stitch
sitting doubly slow I back into death's gentle hippocampus
a surprising emanation without apology
she obeys
she obeys what bleeds casting me in changes or dust-crystal bone
humping on carboned sufferings, feet cold with hunger
sea scratched out, your mouth will swallow my hole in its hole fish
all slick with suchness, reading my body as you do
I bequeath these dirty thoughts to moonbeam and tapered thieves
who jerk off the focus of my hearts and my eggs it's unworldly
to be watery-eyed so hard for you telepathic
joyous I save what was dislodged
internal primal pillows of cardboard realms

[MY SECRET BODY]

The Milky Way is the eye who hides me the body. She desiccates the landscape, sucks liquid from squirrel whose death pinks tarantula cave. In her eye's cloudy forest, other starts scratch out letters to my secret body, caulk them with lipstick and rose oil, hang them in solid air.

Exemptions to her putrid eye are not to be made. For the first time I stand with phosphorescent foxes of midnight chains. We howl in delegation as best we can, forthright murderers, but the cyclical coyotes scoff at our cries. Milky Way pulls her eye from her shoulder to catch a glimpse of other sides. These times are cold. I long for her suctioning kiss. Nebulae hold rich cosmetology: the mask of beating hearts.

Once urban in visage, now powdered glossolalia of ever-functioning earth.

The Milky Way is the eye which overturns justice and conjures entropy. Like climax she cartographizes all form, syllables the world with season and rain, disturbs the inner Milky Way of cellular inscription. All letters wasted, the burn of the pen, the conflagration of focus, imprint of form. Needles belie time.

Glossolalia lives in very different psyches; tinder dry in difference.

there shall be no more cakes, black moon motorcycle
I fuck species for moments across instant penultimate night
fatal fluorescent hard befallen by my own cooked sheath, I will never
rat out anyone
sedition Stratocaster
absence rebels luminous metal flashlight to streetlessly clench
streaming honeydew
butterfly thighborn cosmos, rubber black, a stunning mothership
it's your name in mystic arch, mischief xerox moon, amp of your red
    lobal cortex
hip furrowed in erupted indispensable drool   shall I feed thee
    interminable identities
                                                            such as mine own
all hate sluttery but me I love it

BIRD'S DESTROYER

circumstance portentous
stripped
to
six
melodies
decipher
unladylike dire Empire
plucked across infinite shot

my selves jailors
with blood weather
caterpillar kindling

in custody
with terror
territory haunted—
forest lettered—
bird's destroyer—

FRAILTY

  burned to the dark
        circumference   bell
epigraph
            breathed
             each word
                dripping self
                     over work

  here
       would transfigure
a   mountain   communion   prose
what prison from the gentle
    doubt
        converses
 before her Spark
light has custody of
         famous Grace

   wild sign
whose transport was stolen

    bone licker

no phosphorus   word
would have
been stranger

lips
coup d'état
destruction did alight

Frailty

[MY SECRET BODY]

I stare for a long time, for my secret body to emerge as a scarab. I wrap around the sarcophagus of my selves, tender as a windpipe. My wings, blind eyes, protection—snake bites. When pieces of self emerge, they are changed - one a desert lizard, one a falcon, another a lithe cougar. Another a cottonwood shade, a fire ant mound. Rocks wet.

At twilight, coyotes howl in the cumber bunt of the mountain. It is dawn for my secret body. The wind from the windpipe ushers emeralds lusciously amongst my folded wings.

My body is already a secret. Projected onto Turtle Mountain, the contours of my insect hide fossilize star bindings . . . a cosmological book.

My body is already a secret. Hermetic in canyon thistles. It snores for hours in the gravel. My secret body performs cactus rites, of sap and water.

My secret body is, in part, sympathetic.

what will we have when we look up
shin splints of tears, walls, wounds on fingers, solo
not sweet, not without the openness of a slit
my feathers shriek thru invisibility
ancient gristle on horse tongue
is there anything I can do—I see my double as my double, pressures
of galaxy pushing in, cosmology water, brackish stars
inverts pathetic human body, sea rat with
    indelible overblown artery
cast upon sand, no one made cry but me,
shipwrecked fragile cord   multiplex infant dreamt on
 skulled earth
   there is no use in being up
   what's the use of the couch
these are the times

THE EATER

no longer marked
commanded
pillow proof between
sovereign seconds

myself without bloodshed
gaps in vast chains
composition recluse
crucial present eclipse

the eater
is driven to borders

gun
Fathoms joy
went on to
ethereal tongue

sleep among
Wildness
authoritarian root

day done

  return to Hemispheres

  distance
  money presumption

immovable flying thicket

curse
 tower
  timber
   this
   sunder

fools heart
  in verse

in the Wood: harp

[MY SECRET BODY]

The secret is to be every form and live in every body. The secret is to test your fear of night cougars and stand in the growling dark. Lay on top of the burnished metal car and fry there. The secret is to be a glyph, commotion unto one's self, unclear in the uncool lightbed. The secret is to sleep rock sky bone
    my secret bone made of
            ether and squirrel dust
with nameless insects in ear singing exoskeletal songs
my roots
have fungal mold
it is what the earth is made of
    signal box mold
fascia tunnel folds
    dawn twilight

OPEN SILENCE

open silence

hear the setting
wrecked backwards

more uncertain
watch story
free sweetness
too well lost
you sweep smothered
bitterly, nay, wars
made
furious aspiration
heavy headed sleep

Night aware
in subjective space
abiding—
money owns time
training
her poem
promontory
to rebuke

  ranting House
   relations Hatchet hunting stories
cut off light
                              if you Dare

training
      haunts the land
illusion   holy children
           desolate
           subtraction
    converted
  dozing companion

murderous symbolic sovereign
(once unknown)

meaning the whole sphere I *said licking*
his tongue with my tongue
wolfwild state of matriarchy on
earth fixed identity
froze up as a glacier they have
roots in the cold he didn't answer me
not yet
forms will supplant all unforms
watching Univision
the thunder does not roll in
to overthrow succor, nurturance
not birth, not ESSENCE (forget that!)
all order un-hysterectomied on earth

KILL A THING I WANT

kill a thing I want
      when neighboring doom
unmentioned exiles

         save one House
   violent northern don't you

         swallow sovereign
 firmament Pleasure
reckless as necessity
              some Center
Heights answers
                   monologues

harmony during topography
  part three
     as always
              killed their feathers
  from herself

sang and sang inside
spirit   came among
lines   circumference

blazing
indispensable
recorded
Destroyer

do not mourn among
sisters
suddenly Lilac
in day
Common
Scraps

LETTER AGAINST DISTANCE

dismounted rifle
excavate
wile

Establishment
Universe

letter against Distance
strange fleeing
State into

terse
summer
annihilation

custom:
standing muffled numb

circumference
were voices
known as Eider

rough lyrical
narrative Humans—
death wayward between

[MY SECRET BODY]

When my secret body appears sometimes it ignores me completely and snuffs the grasses with its biennial ass in the air, its pointed face in the ass of the earth, amongst the grubs, the scarab, the moth eggs and the fire ants. Among the most sacred of the land, the reviled and ignored.

When my secret body appears sometimes it is as a jack rabbit whose sequoia ears lift the yellow hand weights of clouds. It hops ferociously forward near a slain tree trunk then halts for many minutes. I don't move my body or head, just my eyes, and it seems to do the same.

My secret body has a plan for me and it is wild.

My secret body is omniscient amid this narrative. Through its eyelet and threads, feathers and furs, skins and stock, minerals, scales, harmonics, highway keys and rogue canyons, my secret body leaps and snorts and grunts and guffaws.

When my secret body appears sometimes it is invisible and wrapped in scarves of wind-body. Sometimes it is invisible and cocooned in the howl and hoot of the whipped mountainside. It is invisible and eats in earthholes, it is invisible and marks me with its thorny sticker.

When my secret body appears sometimes it is invisible and transmogrifies me, a valley of smoke. Secrets a scorpion under my pillow, burns up the coffee pot by forgetting it all day. Writhes me in the dryer after I am laundered. Stairways my name, secret and unfindable.

It is invisible and lays its binocular gaze unto the water storage tank on the hill.

It is invisible and stomps its hooves in the evening tide.

It is invisible and fingers the low barbed brush with ungulates.

When my secret body appears, sometimes it blackly dreams in half my tears, appoints half to me as salt.

Sometimes it is invisible, it's a pawprint of negative space, it's a shitpile of luscious wet berries left behind, invisible as a spoon in the kitchen on which is engraved L.A. COUNTY SCHOOL DISTRICT.

Invisible as raindrop fossilized in packed, indifferent dirt.

Invisible as a color who couldn't hold in ever-shifting sunlight.

[ACKNOWLEDGMENTS]

The author would like to thank Michael Jeffrey Lee, John Coletti, Joseph Bradshaw, Brandon Brown, Alli Warren, Anselm Berrigan, Ariel Resnikoff, Jacob Kahn, Jared Stanley, Laura Woltag and Ted Rees for providing helpful feedback as the work was being written.

Many thanks to The Elephants for bringing this out in the world, and Broc Rossell for his insightful edits and readings of this work as we readied the book.

Pieces of this work have been published at *Castle Grayskull, NoMaterialism*, *The Doris*, *can we have our ball back*, *Elderly*, and *The Brooklyn Rail*. Some of the poems were published as the chapbooks "Detonated Mirror" (Blazing Stadium, 2020) and "Starved Crew" (Eyelet Press, 2021). Thank you to the editors.

Sara Larsen is the author of *The Riot Grrrl Thing* (Roof Books), *Merry Hell* (Atelos Press), and *All Revolutions Will Be Fabulous* (Printing Press)as well as several chapbooks. She was a recipient of a 2021 research grant for non-German literature from the Berlin Senate Department for Culture and Europe. Readings, performances, and publications can be found at *www.saralarsenpoet.com*